SMART RETIREMENT MADE EASY

SMART RETIREMENT MADE EASY

Sam Badgley

Smart Retirement Made Easy

Copyright © 2021 by Sam Badgley

Published by: Bexsi Publishing

All rights reserved.

No part of this book may be reproduced, stored in a retrieval system, or transmitted by any means, electronic, mechanical, photocopying, recording, or otherwise, without written permission from the author.

ISBN-13 :

TABLE OF CONTENTS

Preface 9
Introduction 17

Part 1. Belief System 23
Chapter 1. What Is Money? 25
Chapter 2. Three Myths of Investing 37
Chapter 3. Three Simple Rules of Investing 45

Part 2. Building a plan 53
Chapter 4. Crafting a plan 55
Chapter 5. Let's build the buckets 63
Chapter 6. Putting the buckets together 71

Part 3. Fads, Fears, Facts, and Opinions 79
Chapter 7. Taxes 81
Chapter 8. HSAs 91
Chapter 9. Insurance 95
Chapter 10. Social Security 103
Chapter 11. To ROTH or not to ROTH 111
Chapter 12. Debt 119
Chapter 13. Extra Ingredients 123

Part 4. Next Steps 145
Chapter 14. What is the best way to spend money and time? ... 147
Chapter 15. Should you hire a financial advisor? 153
Chapter 16. Now... The Choice is Yours 159

MY MISSION

I want you to know what you are doing, why you are doing it, how much it costs, and what to expect.

If you know these four things you will be among the most sophisticated investors in the country.

—Sam Badgley

PREFACE

I have been a serial entrepreneur since I was 12 years old. It began with my first paper route. I eventually became a CPA after graduating college.

After being in practice as a CPA for over thirty years, I sat down one day and took stock. What I saw changed my life, the way I practice tax planning and the start of providing retirement planning. Things were going well. I loved my work, I loved my clients and I had a wonderfully successful practice.

I had older clients who had been with me from my beginnings and many clients who were close to my own age. Some were now into their fifties and sixties and things were happening. Many had become friends as well as clients, but only looked to me for fixing or helping with tax preparation or planning. I started to see people I cared about getting older but not prepared for retirement financially.

One of the hardest things working with clients can be delivering bad news: "You will run out of money by age 71 at your current withdrawal rate"..."Your investment portfolio looks suspicious"..."We need to talk about this."

I became increasingly aware that most of these conversations were happening for reasons that were clear and avoidable.

It was not that I missed something or failed to spot a potential issue in their portfolio. I had done what most CPA's in this country do well, which is to provide people with good tax planning and preparation. I began to think I could be providing them with great financial health. I had not made this a primary focus, and far too many clients—including many very smart people—were creating lousy financial lives.

I had further thoughts during this moment of reflection. My relationships with my clients were long-term—twenty or thirty years. That's one of the best things about being a CPA. This privileged, long-term look into clients' lives has put me on a different footing from that of more transactional specialists.

I am aware of how my clients are living. I am aware that the normal American way of retirement is in jeopardy and at risk. And I am aware that, no matter how great the opportunities one has to create a financially secure retirement—fewer people are going to actually get it.

It is inexplicable that our society, plagued by financial pornography, cares so little about these things. The simple fact is that we know perfectly well what to do or if not at least what *not* to do. Around 70% of financial problems are due to lifestyle and poor behavior. If we had the will to do it, we could eliminate more than half of the financial obstacles we face. Not delay it... **eliminate it**. Instead, these invisible problems make them part of the "normal" landscape of our finances. As in, "Oh, that's a normal part of planning for retirement." Let me be honest with you. It is not "normal".

Sadly, we have simply gotten used to this because we have set the bar so shamefully low. A lot of people unconsciously assume these issues will resolve themselves later. People unconsciously assume they will get old and die so it doesn't matter. That is a deeply mistaken idea and dangerous for planning your life. Most Americans are living into their mid-eighties or longer, regardless of health which is another subject matter. That number is rising which is a good reason to make the last third of your life terrific and not financially burdened and miserable.

This was my epiphany. I thought, "I cannot, as a CPA, sit here and watch people I care for, and care about, go down a road that is leading them to an awful place without doing something." I believe this is preventable, so it's my job to prevent it. The good news is that you don't need to wait to do something. This fight can be led, fought and won one person at a time starting with you.

As I have watched clients over the years since that epiphany. I have been struck by how many of them suffer from bad financial advice. That seems to happen a lot these days. The great news is most people get it and become financially healthy.

You also are about to begin your journey. First, let me tell you the story of the most profitable and safely guarded secret in the world.

To begin, there are only a few people in the entire world who know it. It was originally developed in 1940 and the hand-written version of it is protected by a security system created to protect the recipe. Any bandit bent on stealing it would have to maneuver his way through an assortment of high-tech security measures such as motion detectors, cameras, and numerous armed guards that monitor and surround the vault where it is kept.

What is this incredibly guarded secret that I am referring to? If you said Coca Cola you would be close, but no cigar. The most heavily guarded secret is actually the 11 secret herbs and spices that make up Colonel Sanders' Original Recipe chicken that is still used at Kentucky Fried Chicken today!

The chicken recipe is such a tightly guarded secret that only two company executives at any one time have access to it. Moreover, KFC uses multiple suppliers for each ingredient so each supplier is only privy to a small part of the 11 ingredient recipe.

Many have attempted to copy Colonel Sanders' incredibly profitable recipe, yet all have failed to come up with the correct proportions of the 11 secret ingredients. Rumor has it that all 11 secret ingredients can be found right in your local grocery store. There is not a single ingredient that is rare or tough to find for the average consumer....yet not a single person in 81 years has figured it out.

Of course if you've ever tried to duplicate a recipe, you know that it isn't as easy as it seems. People continue to attempt to duplicate KFC because it's one of the best and most profitable recipes in the world. It's the secret responsible for making KFC millions upon millions of dollars and has even resulted in a company valued at multiple billions of dollars.

Some irony to the secret is that even though 11 ingredients are readily available to any consumer in America, 99% of us would rather have the convenience of pulling up to the local KFC and getting hot chicken fast, versus doing it all on our own. I would be willing to bet that even if the secret ingredients and exact recipe were indeed leaked out, the vast majority of Americans would still prefer to walk in or pull up to the local KFC and buy their chicken. And quite candidly most people don't care what the ingredients are, they just want it to taste good!

Now you are probably asking yourself what all this has to do with you and investing? I mean, you are looking for financial advice—not crispy chicken.

Well the same principle above for chicken relates to investing. We don't really care what the investing ingredients are, we just want it to work, right? Yes and no. I am here to tell you that investing can be just as easy as making a fried chicken leg… but with one little catch.

You have to know the ingredients and the systems to make it work.

But before we get started, I do have one piece of bad news. This silver bullet investing secret is very similar to KFC in that it comprises many different basic investment ingredients. Meaning, there does not exist just one super-secret ingredient that solves all of your problems. If someone tells you there is, they are mistaken or lying.

However, the super exciting news is that you can count the ingredients on both hands. And the good news is that I just happen to have all the ingredients and the recipe. You just have to be willing to read this book and begin to implement them. Some will ask, "Why would you share your secret recipe? What's in it for you?"

Simple. Many Americans still prefer to walk in or pull up to the local KFC and buy their chicken. If this is you I still want you to understand the ingredients and know why your chicken tastes so good. Let's begin the journey.

INTRODUCTION

I have purposefully kept this book brief and to the point. We need a simpler way to invest. We need to feel confident we are investing prudently and making smart financial decisions. If you feel this book offers nothing new, you would be right. If you think it is too basic, I would suggest the possibility that what you may be looking for either doesn't matter or doesn't exist.

Financial planning is a science of choice. Very few household families have the resources to:

- Maintain all the emergency cash reserves they'd like
- Own all the life, disability, and long-term care insurance they need
- Save all the money to pay for their children's education

- And still invest as much as they need for a dignified, independent retirement

Let's face it. Money is complicated. You may have the best intentions to prepare well for your future, but without a plan *and* a commitment to stay the course, you simply won't get the results you want.

You will find a simpler way to invest in this book.

I hope to provide you with passionate, ethical and empathetic support in this journey. You must make intelligent choices using finite resources. But don't worry, I'm here to help you make better choices and avoid any pitfalls. For instance, consider the stories below I commonly come across. You may relate to a few of them.

Rick and Jane work with a broker who invested their money in some of the firms' popular products. They have no idea how the investments work or what they are paying in fees. They have never talked about a plan to meet their goals and so they are not sure if they are on track. The broker is now recommending a gold fund because of talk about rising inflation. Rick and Jane don't know what to do.

Jen has never trusted the stock market. She and her late husband always invested in CD's and money market funds. She realizes her accounts have not grown very much and probably won't help maintain her current lifestyle. Her local bank is recommending fixed index annuities giving her guarantees but she thinks they are confusing and is suspicious. She is not sure where to turn next.

Fred and Brenda manage their own money through a brokerage account. Fred has made some good picks, but for the most part he really doesn't know how well his portfolio has done. He spends a lot of time on this, yet he knows that he's not really getting anywhere. He worries that if something happens to him, his wife may be put in a tough spot.

Dan has been contributing regularly to his 401(k) plan. After the stock market dropped in 2008, he sold everything in a panic and has been sitting in cash ever since. He wants to retire in the next ten years and wonders what he can do. He wonders if he is just not cut out to be an investor and is doomed to work until he dies.

I want to change the way you think about investing. Wall Street and the financial services industry makes investing so complicated and frightening. **My goal in this book is to empower you to learn *and* understand everything you need to know so you can take control of your financial future!** This venture will not always be easy but I will help make it simple.

There are numerous other books and information that address the ideas you are about to read here, and in much greater detail. However, therein lies part of the problem. For most of us, these publications are too long and frankly too technical. My goal is to express in simple terms the most important concepts in a way any investor can understand. And that focuses on the things we can control.

I have organized this book into four parts. The first part is your belief system. The saying goes if you believe in nothing you will eventually believe in anything. You must have a foundation built upon solid rock for everything else to work.

The second part will teach you how to build your plan. How to determine how much money you will need and how to develop an accumulation as well as a distribution strategy once you achieve success.

The third part addresses fears, fads, facts, and opinions where we discuss a lot of common industry jargon and strategies. You will find some warnings as well as clarification on importance. The investment industry often likes to distract us with things that are not necessarily wrong but can make things more difficult than they need to be.

The fourth part of the book kind of comes full circle to help you determine if you need professional help and what you should look for if you do. Your next steps.

At one point, I wasn't even happy with my own retirement progress. So, I set out in 2010 to help people as well as myself. My goal was to be financially independent in ten years. I have used this book's philosophy and formula as well as strategies to achieve this goal.

Now I want to share my knowledge and experience with you. I am currently more selective and only taking on one out of every four or five prospects I meet with. This leaves a lot of people that still need help. I want to "pay it forward" by sharing this information.

Are you ready to begin your journey? I hope so! I am glad you're here. You must make intelligent choices using finite resources. I hope to provide you with passionate, ethical, and empathetic support as you pursue your financial goals.

Download the toolkit (including all the worksheets) for free! For your bonuses, go to: www.smartretirementmadesimple.com

PART I

BELIEF SYSTEM

CHAPTER 1

WHAT IS MONEY?

In the book of Genesis, God gives Adam and Eve dominion over all the earth, forbidding them only from eating from the tree of the knowledge of good and evil. For a brief moment, their innocence was perfect.

Now being only human, the serpent convinces them to bite into the apple. This is the original transgression, everything bad about earthly life comes rushing into the world. Their eyes were opened but unfortunately to sin, shame, heartache, sickness, and death. They made just one mistake, but it was the only one they were forbidden to do.

Successful investing is a lot like earthly paradise. Done right, long-term investing can simply align with the most cherished lifetime goals of a family. As long as the portfolio remains a servant of a plan, harmony reigns.

But then, being only human, we begin to hear the noise of the serpent of markets, who says: *you can beat this thing. You're smart, you don't have to be tied to simple disciplines like asset allocation and diversification. You can outperform.*

When we bite into the apple of performance—when the focus of our beliefs weakens and digress from our financial goals and into the market itself, we commit the original investment sin. The illusion of consistently superior selection and timing has crept into your garden to destroy you.

We need to build a foundation and belief system around what money is. We must develop the faith, patience, and discipline to dress and keep our garden to avoid the behavioral mistakes our human tendencies create. Lacking these three qualities will prevent you from any peace of mind.

Money is the single most powerful tool we have navigating this complex world we live in. Understanding it is critical. You must choose between you mastering money or money mastering you.

I want to teach you important truths. For example, "complex investments exist only to create profits for those who create and sell them." Further, not only are they more costly to the investor, but they are also less effective. You will also learn the most dangerous obstacle to building wealth is debt.

Wealth is freedom. When your investments help provide you a sufficient income to live a full and joyful life, then you are truly wealthy—because you are truly free.

This book will guide you towards financial independence. It is about buying you financial freedom. Putting you in control of your financial destiny.

You will learn steps to financial freedom and how to get your debt under control. Then you will have money to shift into investments and develop strategic tax reduction and planning strategies.

You will hear over and over my mantra: Spend less than you earn, invest the surplus, and avoid debt. This is not always easy. Simple, yes. Easy, no.

Investing really is simple. But if you are paying too much attention to all the gurus, you may be feeling a bit confused, overwhelmed, and uncertain about which strategies to follow. This is why you are reading this book.

What I want you to do right now is get rid of all the noise. Set it all aside. Let's focus on the simple truths about what it takes to grow and protect your investments.

I do not suggest this process will be easy, though the principles and methods in this book are simple, it will perhaps be a challenge to faithfully implement it. The systems in this book require no special expertise and demands extraordinarily little of your time and energy. However, there is no magic formula.

You're likely to exclaim, "Yeah, this isn't rocket science. Tell me something everybody else doesn't know… like (magic bullet)."

You're absolutely right! However, chances are you're not currently following these simple steps or overlooking the value and benefits in the simplicity. I invite you to step forward and take action. Align yourself with the following beliefs and values as you build your financial foundation.

To begin, we need to firmly develop and move toward a philosophy of money and markets and understand how they work. My mission statement has four parts. Two of them deal with philosophy, particularly 1) knowing what you are doing and 2) why you are doing it.

For instance, are there consistent principles or laws that an investor can be guided by or is the economic and financial universe utterly random? You cannot make an investment policy out of chaos, so we need to nail this down. If order rather than chaos is the first principle of capital markets the second must be "if it isn't simple, it isn't true."

The complexities, manifold though they may be, are just refinements. All—not some—of the critical decisions the lifetime investor must make are simple. This is where human nature gets in the way.

So, what is money?

The reason this is so important is because most Americans do not know the answer. Each person I described in the introduction situation can easily be traced to this principle.

People think that money is denominated by the number of units in their currency. If they had one million dollars twenty years ago, and still have one million dollars today, they believe they have preserved their money and kept it safe. The problem is they have lost half their purchasing power through even moderate inflation.

This tells us that in the long run the only logical, clear definition of money is purchasing power. Successful long-term investing must first be the maintenance and increase of purchasing power. This realization kicks off the discussion of beliefs and patterns which will lead to wealth.

The human impulse is to protect the number of currency units. This impulse will almost invariably result in a negligible return net of inflation and a negative real return after ordinary income taxation.

Currency is not money, because its purchasing power is always declining. Investing for retirement is the process of putting away today's dollars to realize more money (greater purchasing power) in the future. Now we can begin to support this structure.

For at least the last ninety years, an authoritative history of returns from Ibbotson/Morningstar, small company stocks have compounded at about twelve percent. Large company stocks have compounded at around ten percent.

Now the plot thickens. Over this same period of time, long-term, high-quality corporate bonds have compounded at about six percent. Clearly, the practice of owning companies (small and large company stocks) yielded significantly higher returns than lending to companies (Bonds).

Consumer inflation compounded at three percent during this same period. In terms of how we measure returns, stocks earned well over twice that of bonds. What should interest you is the relationship. At least historically, equities or stocks have been far more effective in growing your purchasing power than bonds.

Keep in mind this all occurs over nine decades. Quite a long time. During that time all kinds of wars, booms, recessions, and pandemics occurred many times over. The point of this story reveals another question: why do efficient markets pay twice, in real terms, what it paid the bondholder? The investor's default answer is "risk."

The good news is risk is the chance of permanent loss of capital. *A permanent or even semi-permanent decline has never happened*. Let me repeat that, "a permanent or even semi-permanent decline has never happened."

Equity values have certainly declined sharply on many occasions and should be expected to do so again and again as well as risen sharply. The net effect of all these declines and advances produced the results we just reviewed.

It would appear that, at least historically, the risk of permanent loss in a broadly diversified equity portfolio is not merely a misunderstanding, but a myth. We will soon speak of more investing myths but for now where does this current myth come from?

First, many investors have inherited this fear from previous generations or bad experiences from their past. Investors need to remember stocks are merely shares of companies that represent direct ownership of the earnings, cash flow and net assets of businesses which they themselves patronize regularly.

Stocks are investments. Not speculation like casino chips. A constantly rising trend line results even though the seasonal market cycle waxes and wanes. We need to avoid the emotional overreaction to such developments.

The twenty-four-hour news cycle perpetuates this fear. The financial news cycle is, very deliberately, a culture of fear. It has no interest in reporting the truth. The culture of language from the news media has promoted stocks as "aggressive" and bonds as "conservative." Conventional wisdom further identifies bonds as providing "safe income" and stocks as "risky growth."

I consider myself a conservative investor defined as one intent on preserving my money and increasing my purchasing power. However, I am determined to leave money to the people I love.

Too often when people ignore these principles and panic, they will blame "the stock market." Others will simply have one bad experience and try to learn too much from it, rather than taking personal responsibility.

My mission and value proposition is to keep people from blowing themselves up. We have openly discussed the

Big Mistake—the fatal inability to distinguish risk from mere volatility. Follow and understand these principles because markets don't create loss, The investor does.

Genuine panic that can take the equity market down by a third requires three conditions. First, we must be experiencing a national or global financial/economic trend/event which no one can understand. Second, the majority must conclude that the "crisis" is insoluble. The third is, "this time is different."

I would argue this can only happen if history no longer applies. In that case, nothing really matters anyway. Once you accept this premise, we now must define volatility. After all, this is the premium an investor receives for taking on the unpredictability of holding stocks.

Simply put, if you can't endure upwards of a fifteen percent intra-year decline every year, and an average decline of about a third one year in five, you are just flat-out too squeamish and can never be an equity investor. Remember, of course, that these are always temporary, and the trend line is always growing long-term.

This is where the Wall Street bullies capitalize on weak investors, wanting them to think alternative investments exist without volatility—which is just a lie. *Anything that suppresses volatility also suppresses returns significantly.*

If you have stuck with me to this point, congratulations. This chapter is the hardest one but particularly important. Dealing with conventional wisdom and human nature particularly from the emotional side can be difficult and a little confusing. To the extent we can prepare for and prevent surprises, we may head off panic.

You may even want to re-read this chapter. Especially if you are feeling a little anxious about the markets. **You need to feel this philosophy and principles in your bones.** You must formulate this philosophy, as distinctly opposed to reacting with an outlook. A true philosophy never changes in response to current events.

There is an appropriate old adage: *time* in the market—as opposed to **timing** the market—is the key to capturing the superior returns of equities (stock market).

As we close this chapter keep in mind this powerful fact concerning returns the next time you feel an itch to panic and think "this time is different." With dividends reinvested, in all rolling one-year periods (with a new period starting each month) since 1926, equity returns have been positive seventy-four percent of the time.

But at five years, the positive percentage leaps to eighty-seven percent. At ten years, it is ninety-four percent and when we get out to fifteen years, it's statistically as close to 100% as you can get: There are only two rolling fifteen-year periods of negative returns out of something like nine-hundred and counting. Let that sink in a bit.

Let's move to the next two chapters to learn some more about myths and rules of investing.

CHAPTER 2

THREE MYTHS OF INVESTING

I believe investors intuitively believe and take some investment concepts for granted as being good advice. When you talk about investment advice with stockbrokers and traditional financial advisors, the most common questions tend to follow such as:

1. What stocks or investments do you like?
2. What 5-star funds do you prefer?
3. Where do you think the market is going?

You may not realize these questions actually ask for a prediction about how your investments will perform in the future—something that's not really possible to predict.

So, if this is what an investor is looking for in investment advice, shouldn't we test these beliefs to see if they really work? Let's take a closer look at what I call "Financial Planning Myths."

MYTH #1: STOCK PICKING

This investment approach is based on someone being able to pick stocks that will do well in the future. Unfortunately, an investment advisor can't consistently and predictably add value to your portfolio through individual stock picking.

Amazingly, many funds turn out to be duds. What do you think happens to those funds? They disappear to avoid reporting the bad results. The industry does not want you to know stock picking is a myth. A total of over 68,707 funds have been created.

Today around 32,000 exist. What happened to the other 36,000 including the return data? These funds that underperform are either killed or merged into more successful funds to hide the real truth.

It is a challenge for smart people to accept they can't pick and outperform an index that simply buys everything. Let me be absolutely clear. I don't favor indexing just because it's easier, although it is. Or because it is simpler, although it is that too. *I favor it because it is more effective and more powerful in building wealth than any other alternative.*

MYTH #2: TRACK RECORD INVESTING

This myth uses historic performance to determine the best investments for future performance. The belief is that by finding stocks who have performed well in the past will allow the investor to determine which funds will do well in the future. The star ratings for many funds perpetuate this theory as well.

Unfortunately, past performance has zero correlation to future performance. You can look at even short five-year periods and rarely do the top 30 mutual funds for that time period repeat in the following five-year period. A portfolio manager's ability to pick stocks in the past has little to no correlation with his/her ability to do so consistently in the future.

MYTH #3: MARKET TIMING

This is an attempt to alter or change the mix of assets based on a forecast or prediction of the future. Money managers believe they can predict the future. You can listen to the TV or radio every day and understand what I am saying.

DALBAR is an independent research firm that measures investor behavior. They look at the real results investors get from the markets. During more than 30-year time periods the S&P 500 has returned about 9.96% while the average equity investor's return was only 5.04%. The results are directly from getting in and out of the market as one attempts to time the ups and downs.

He goes into his investments, and then sells out of them, at the wrong time and for the wrong reasons. Missing these top days can prove costly. If you had an investment from July 1, 2000 to June 30, 2020, but was out of the market only 10 days of the total 20 years or 7300 days you would have ended with half as much money.

Why would you be likely to miss the best days? Because these days occurred within two weeks of a worst day

70 percent of the time and they occurred within six months of a best day 100 percent of the time! This proves easily how market timing is a risky proposition. The frightening part is market timing can be disguised and most investors don't realize they are victims.

To summarize these three myths, keep this in mind: The economy is entirely uncorrelated to the markets over any but the very longest time horizons. So even if you knew what the economy was going to do next—and you can't—you'd still have no idea what the markets would do.

Never ask the economy what the markets are going to do. The economy won't even tell you what it's going to do. Economic forecasting is another loser's game.

Now that you have heard the three myths of investing you might wonder if there is a way to avoid these myths. I'm glad you asked. Nobel prize winners, authors and leading academics serve as the foundation and basis for countering these common industry myths.

The first major principle is that free markets work. In simple terms this means that in a free market the price of a security will be a good estimate of its intrinsic value. This is an important part of the belief system we discussed previously.

This belief confirms that free markets are the best determinant of market prices based on supply and demand. Only new and unknowable information and events will change the price in the future.

This makes it impossible for any individual or entity to consistently predict market movements and capture additional returns unrelated to risk.

It is important to believe in an efficient market hypothesis in that nobody can pick or predict markets. Once you have this core belief, we can move on to Modern Portfolio Theory.

Harry Markowitz won the Nobel prize for portfolio design and risk reduction. Essentially his theory helps build a portfolio for the greatest return for a given risk tolerance in the most efficient way.

This theory proves when building a portfolio diversification and particularly utilizing assets with low correlation is one of the best ways to reduce risk in your portfolio. Mr. Markowitz was way ahead of his time. It took nearly 40 years for computer technology to prove this theory.

The value of Modern Portfolio Theory is it helps you create an optimal portfolio. This method increases return while reducing volatility. This can easily be measured but is often overlooked.

The third factor coincidentally is the three-factor model. The three-factor model explains 97% of the variability of returns. These factors determine which sources of risk the market rewards with higher returns. The three risk factors are: The Market Factor, The Size Factor, and The Value Factor.

The Three Factor Model makes it possible to calculate expected returns based on these risk factors. In sum, the Three-Factor Model tells us that the market is expected to reward investors for taking risks, especially in equities, a bit more for small companies, and even a bit more for distressed companies.

These three methods eliminate the need to rely on these traditional myths of investing and follow a better academic based approach to investing based on science not luck. Every investor seeks the opportunity to achieve true investing peace of mind.

Most importantly make sure your portfolio is designed with prudent risks that have expected historic premiums and academically sound design.

I use a Portfolio Diagnostic Report to help create, measure, and compare a portfolio for optimization. This report help make three crucial decisions creating the opportunity to productively apply these methods while avoiding the myths to your portfolio:

- How much of my portfolio am I going to put in Equities versus Fixed Income?
- How should I allocate between Small Stocks versus Large Stocks?
- How should I allocate to Value Stocks versus Growth Stocks?

These three decisions based on academic research will account for 95% of the portfolio's returns (performance).

In the next chapter, I'll present three simple rules for investing. Once you understand these rules, you'll be ready for the next step: building a plan.

CHAPTER 3

THREE SIMPLE RULES OF INVESTING

I am going to share the three simple rules of investing:

Rule #1: Own Equities

Rule #2: Diversify Globally

Rule #3: Rebalance

RULE #1 OWN EQUITIES

I believe you must hold at least a portion of your wealth in equity-based mutual funds. There are generally two types of investments that make up a portfolio: Equities (or stocks) and Fixed Income (bonds).

The decision of what percentage of each of these investments to hold will be the primary determinant of your investment performance. Clearly stocks have a higher risk/return versus bonds lower risk/return. As a matter of fact, stocks tend to outpace bond returns historically by about two to one as we learned in Chapter 1.

This asset allocation decision goes a little further than just the equity and fixed income percentage breakdown. Once you decide how the breakdown of each class can be further broken down within the category—such as cash, US government bonds, municipal bonds, and corporate bonds on the fixed side and US large value, growth, small, International, and emerging markets—then you will complete a more diversified portfolio. These additional classes provide ways to give weightings to each, reducing volatility and risk while improving returns.

Keep in mind that risk and return are related. In the investment world, the most widely used measure of risk is standard deviation which is a statistical measure of the degree to which annual returns of an investment differ from their average. Under normal circumstances, about two thirds of the returns fall within one standard deviation of the average.

One way to explain this is to consider two different investments with different risk/return characteristics (or asset allocations). For example, Fund A is a heavily weighted bond portfolio with an expected average return of four percent with an expected standard deviation of two percent.

This means that about two-thirds of the time, this investment is expected to return between two percent and six percent (plus or minus two percent). Fund B, a heavily weighted equity portfolio, has a higher expected return of 10 percent, but also a higher expected standard deviation of 20 percent, meaning that about two-thirds of the time Fund B should return between 30 percent and -10 percent (plus or minus 20 percent).

Clearly an investment in Fund B would entail more risk than Fund A. Every investor should know the standard deviation or risk/return of their portfolio and the possible returns the portfolio will generate to make sure they can accept the outcome and not panic at an inopportune time. My Portfolio Diagnostic Report can help measure any portfolio's standard Deviation *(for more information, contact my office at 1-304-375-3843)*.

Research by Dalbar tells us the average investor only holds their equity mutual funds for approximately three years causing returns to be less than two thirds of the actual market return due to panic and impatience.

Just remember: the higher the standard deviation the more volatile the risk. Also remember a mix of some fixed income with your equity can actually reduce the volatility and impact the overall risk of your portfolio in a positive way.

RULE #2 GLOBAL DIVERSIFICATION

In simple terms this means don't put all your eggs in one basket. Most people would agree with this statement but how many baskets do you need? Many investors are confused and believe owning a lot of stuff is diversification—not true.

Most times all the funds own the same companies. We call this overlap. It turns out that the asset allocation and classes we discussed previously can be positively correlated, uncorrelated or negatively correlated. These differences in correlation creates a blended portfolio with lower volatility (lower standard deviation).

An important component of financial economists is called Modern Portfolio Theory. This important concept of my philosophy was introduced in 1952 by Nobel Laureate Harry Markowitz as we mentioned him previously.

It underscores the importance of focusing on the performance of your portfolio, rather than the returns of the individual components. The bottom line is some asset classes will not do as well as others. Therefore, owning all the markets is so important.

The more your portfolio is diversified in many different companies in many different industries, the less your financial goal is dependent on your or anyone else's ability to successfully pick individual stocks, industries, or trends—something money managers have proven is not easily done.

This is why I propose indexing your portfolio. With the help of today's sophisticated computer programs, an advisor can access the historical risk and return data to help construct a diversified portfolio.

This narrows down the selection process allowing you to own the whole market Domestically and Internationally and identify the funds that give you the widest selection of companies in the maximum number of industries.

A well-constructed portfolio will consist of US Large Company Growth, US Large Company Value, US Small Company Growth, US Small Company Value, International Large Growth and Value, International Small Growth and Value at a minimum for the equity percentage of the portfolio.

This combination will give you over 14,000 companies in over 45 Countries. That's diversification.

RULE #3 REBALANCING

The simple definition of rebalancing is what results when markets happen and the portfolio drifts away from the original allocation we created when you built the portfolio. The different classes, as we learned, will move differently. Some up, some down and at various rates. These changes will cause the allocation percentages to change from our target allocation.

For example, if equity markets enjoy a period of strong returns, it is possible that a 60-40 stock/bond portfolio could drift to a 70-30 mix. Left alone, your portfolio will have a higher risk level at what could be a market high point.

By rebalancing back to the 60-40 mix you started with, you can maintain your desired level of risk and expected return. This is not always easy to do.

In the above example, rebalancing is accomplished by either adding new money in lump sum or from a regular systematic contribution you set up to the fixed side, withdrawing from the equity side if you are taking distributions, or by selling some of the equities and reinvesting the proceeds into the fixed income to bring you back to 60-40.

You have now essentially bought low and sold high without your emotions getting in the way.

Rebalancing in a tax deferred account is easy because you are not subject to a capital gains tax on profits taken. A regular taxable account can impact taxes so consideration when rebalancing should be made.

Fear not, there are many fund companies like Vanguard that have tax efficient funds as well as other strategies to minimize any potential tax impact. The exercise of rebalancing is still effective and will provide higher returns.

The whole concept of rebalancing is one of the value drivers an advisor can help the investor navigate when constructing and managing a portfolio.

To recap, you should rebalance your portfolio because it controls risk over time, it prevents panicking and buying/selling asset categories at the wrong time, and it ensures a systematic process of buying low and selling high.

PART II

BUILDING A PLAN

CHAPTER 4

CRAFTING A PLAN

Be keenly aware that goals are not plans. Before I craft a plan for a client, I need to address some important points. Because financial planning is a science of choices.

Very few families have the resources to address the infinite options with the finite resources they possess. We plan to protect our families because nobody intentionally wants to leave their family lacking.

You need to accumulate a sum of capital between now and your retirement so you can withdraw a steadily increasing and therefore lifestyle-sustaining stream of withdrawals while still leaving substantial legacies for your children and grandchildren. That's our challenge. That's the scope of where we are now headed.

This process consists of two phases: the accumulation phase and distribution phase. We start by making an effort to estimate what your monthly expenses will most likely be in the first 12 months you're retired. Some people will use their current spending as a start.

You also may adjust for the expectation that at retirement you will be debt-free and will not be contributing to your retirement plan. This leads some people to use, as an example, 75-80% of their current spending.

Be realistic at this stage. We can always tweak the numbers later. Better to be realistic than to deceive yourself with unrealistic numbers. A retirement where you sit and stare at a TV screen is not a very healthy way to spend your retirement years.

The number you arrive at will be what we need to withdraw from your investments after accounting for what you will be getting from Social Security and any other income you can expect from a pension, rental income or other additional source.

Now since you are not retiring today: you're retiring (x) years from now we need to inflate this number for inflation. If inflation is say 3% and you need $50,000 today, then in 10 years that amount will be approximately $67,000*.

Next, we need to gross that number up for taxation. Keep in mind you will need $67,000 for expenses but we will need to pay the tax man first.

For this pass through let's assume a tax rate of 15%. This equates to taking out ten years from now approximately $79,000 to pay 15% in taxes and be left with $67,000 to cover expenses after inflating today's $50,000 expenses.

Take a minute to review each of the steps we took in order to make an estimate of your pre-tax withdrawal need 10 years from now. Now we can determine what sum of capital must we accumulate to support that withdrawal. I recommend a formula of 4.5% in the first year and escalating the amount 3% each year to offset inflation.

We can debate this method or one of many other philosophies but remember we are going someplace you have never been, and we will have time to crunch the numbers. I also recommend a couple years living expenses that you will want set aside from the bulk investments in case you need to shut off your withdrawals from the investment portion in case of a market downturn particularly in the early retirement years (sequence of returns).

*Use the following formula to inflation adjust your spending needs: $R = C \times (I + 1)T$

R = Spending needs C = Today's dollars I = Projected inflation T = Number of years until retirement

So, your targeted $79,000 calculated earlier is 4.5% of $1.7 million (round numbers). Add roughly another $160,000 in reserve, and you're at $1.9 million. That's the dollar amount you'd have to accumulate 10 years from now.

Does this method of calculating your capital need at retirement make sense to you?

The third and final step in this process we need to solve is what monthly investment amount you need to make to fill any gap we found from our previous calculations.

The first step is to determine how much money you have put away specifically for retirement up to this point. You need to be realistic of what sum of money you can reasonably commit to invest in each and every one of the next 120 months (ten years)

As an example, say you currently have $750,000 in an IRA. If we assume a rate of return of 8%, we will need to invest $1500 per month for 120 months and keep the $750,000 invested to earn the same 8% and we would end up with $1.9 million. Hooray! You are ready to retire.

Keep in mind this is just an example. Substitute your own numbers to calculate for your specific situation. Knowing your number is very critical to the process.

The happy day comes and now we only must make a few simple decisions. First, will we need any money for large capital expenditures in the first five years? If so, we will set that aside in a money market type fund separated from the other dollars.

Next, we set aside those two years of living expenses I mentioned previously. This is for protection against potential market setbacks early in your retirement.

The balance of the invested wealth will be in a broadly diversified equity portfolio following the principles and guidelines you have been learning. Now you can begin drawing the 4.5% in the first year and increasing it by 3% per year to offset inflation.

In the long run, the balance of your portfolio would be compounding at an assumed rate of 8-10%. So, I think you can see that, over time (although not every single year) your withdrawals should fall further and further in the line of your portfolio value.

Now that we have created the plan calculating the needed capital sum at retirement and formulating a sufficiently robust investing program for accumulating the sum, we have two steps left to complete the program.

The first, create an investment policy statement recognizing the appropriate asset mix and allocation necessary to reach the capital sum in the allotted time we calculated. Then secondly, create the portfolio itself.

The important thing to remember is that the Investment Policy Statement for both the accumulation phase and distribution phase is essentially a commitment of the previous conceptual agreements you made with yourself.

There can be no assurance of your achieving the required returns in the next ten years or even that the strategy will succeed. You will be required to review these strategies at least annually, but provided the goals have not changed, you should not expect to alter materially your plan or your portfolio.

Now you can utilize the plan and investment policy statement to create the portfolio based on the many fundamentals and principles discussed throughout this book.

Let's move on and build the buckets.

CHAPTER 5

LET'S BUILD THE BUCKETS

Now that we know how much we need to save each month, we are ready to build out our portfolio. You may already have some of the buckets from any current portfolio you have. You can use chapter 6 to better align these dollars with the principles we have been learning.

I developed a waterfall approach that makes the first part of the decision fairly easy. In our previous example of crafting our plan, we determined we needed to save $1500 per month.

Let's take it another step and say we wanted to save 25%. Remember savings rate is more important than return rate. A couple earning $175,000 would then be saving $43,750 or a tad over $3,645 per month.

We will start at the top of the waterfall and work down:

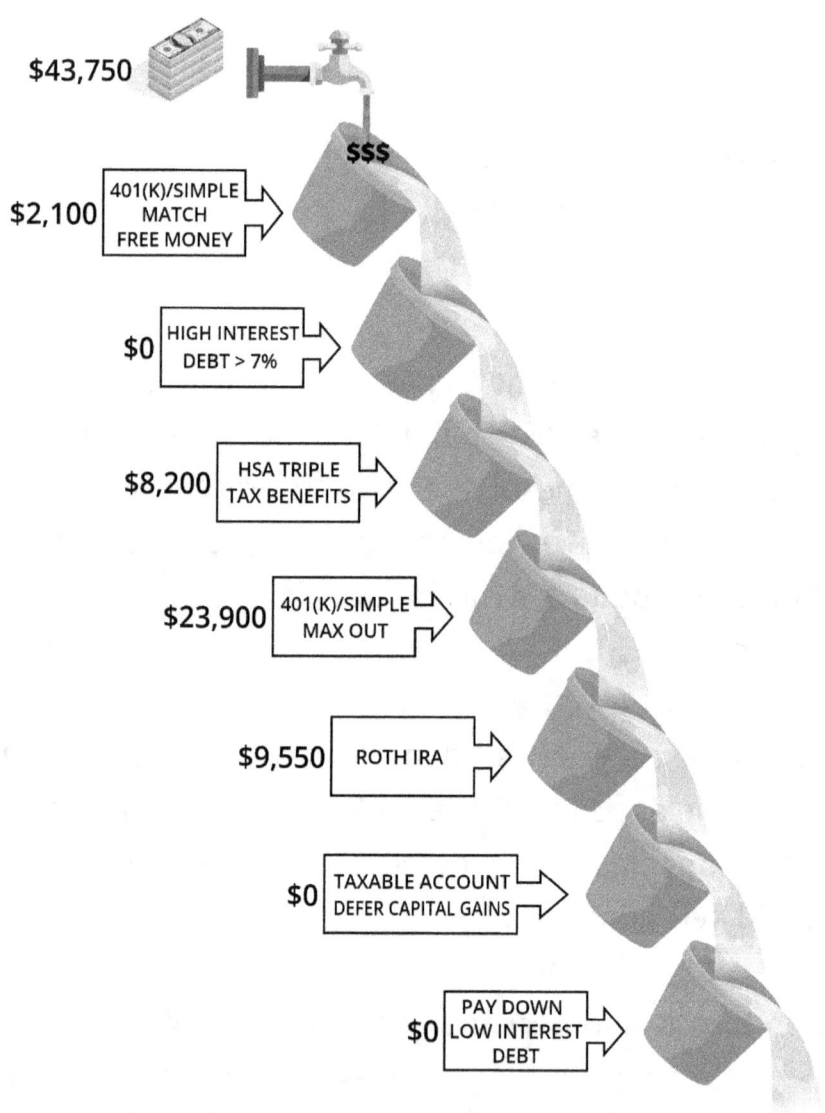

I like to describe each of the above as different buckets for the different retirement account options. Once again, I will remind you that at this stage, we should already have an emergency fund. Proper insurance also needs to be in place.

The idea behind this process is to fill up the buckets in the order listed. Your specific circumstances may change some things, but this should serve as a good rule of thumb. Here are some explanations of why the order is important.

We start the waterfall by making sure you claim free money from any matching contributions in employer retirement plans.

Next, I recommend paying down high interest debt. I would consider anything over 7% and particularly 10% as high interest. Credit cards would be the most obvious example. The reason is this is a guaranteed return that positively impacts your net worth immediately.

Folks with high deductible health plans, which are increasingly common, a health savings account (HSA) has triple-tax benefits that makes this a great long-term retirement vehicle.

Contributions are deductible on front end, grow tax free, and withdrawals are tax free if used for health expenses. I personally contribute to an HSA but pay my medical expenses out of pocket and retain the receipt as proof so that during retirement I have the option to withdraw the money and not be required to use it for health care expenses, although it's likely I will have more health expenses in retirement.

Next, I recommend maxing out your pre-tax contributions to qualified retirement plans 401(k)'s, 403(b)'s, 457,'s or SIMPLE IRA plans. Younger people might consider 401(k) ROTH options if available particularly if you are in a lower tax bracket (<24%).

You now would look at contributing to ROTH IRA's either directly or through "backdoor" if over the income limits (of $196,000-$206,000 in Adjusted Gross Income for married tax filers in 2020). Before moving further down make sure you've explored any other tax-advantaged accounts that might be available.

High earners and super savers will eventually run out of pre-tax deductions at this point and so you now should create a regular taxable account using tax efficient index mutual funds or ETF funds that don't generate large capital gains.

After you have added some money to a taxable account to be used later in retirement to reduce your taxable income when taking withdrawals, you should consider making extra principal payments on any lower interest debt. There is great psychological value in slaying debt.

You may remember our married couple that needed to acquire enough money to be able to withdraw $79,000 in ten years. Let's jump forward after we implemented the above bucket strategy and now discuss which buckets we now pull our money from in order to reach our needed $79,000.

Here are the critical points to absorb. Most people never reach a 25% level of savings. You can clearly see that until you reach this level you do not need to worry about complicated and magical investment products Savings rate is more important than return rate).

Very basic, simple low-cost investments will get you to your goal. Lastly, by accumulating enough money in your buckets, you will not need to draw more than

4.5% each year. As a result, you will likely never run out of money before you run out of life.

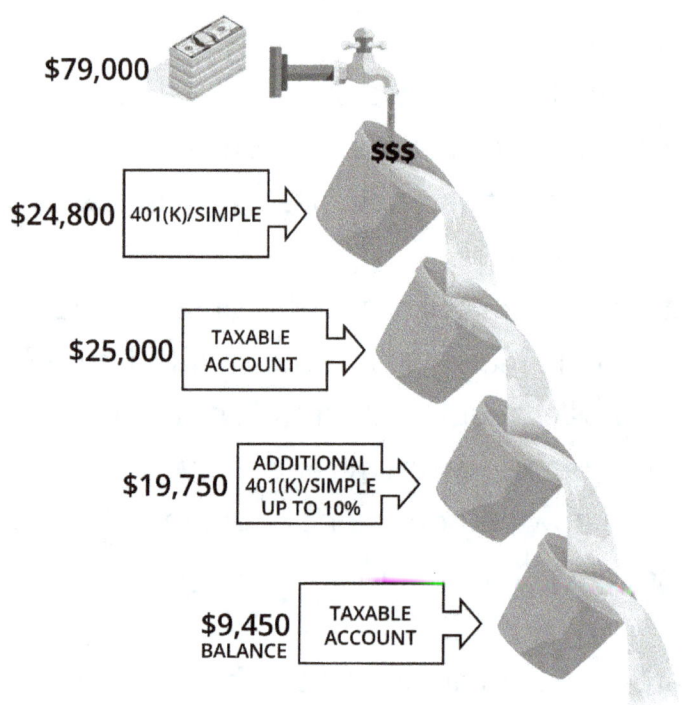

Keep in mind there is nothing magic about this bucket withdrawal plan. The purpose is to try and minimize taxes while maintaining a strict 4.5% withdrawal rate.

You may be more comfortable retaining your taxable account. You can pay more taxes now and then use the taxable account for larger unexpected expenses and avoid creating a higher tax liability.

This is a perfect example where having an advisor to analyze these scenarios can be invaluable. To recap, I demonstrated a bucket strategy to create different buckets to put the required savings in to meet your long-term goal. Our example actually used the example of saving 25% of their salary.

The second part was the withdrawal strategy after ten years of accumulation and our couple retired. Which buckets we take our money out of using a 4.5% withdrawal rate and minimizing taxes was illustrated.

Now, let's next figure out what you actually buy with each of the buckets of money.

CHAPTER 6

PUTTING THE BUCKETS TOGETHER

After determining your asset allocation, we are only left with which funds to purchase with our buckets of money. You may need to review the asset allocation part again but please don't let it hold you up.

A very popular allocation particularly for people not confident with the stock market would be a 60% equity and 40% fixed allocation. We will use this allocation in our example but feel free to be more aggressive or conservative if you prefer. The fundamentals will not change.

As an advisor I have access to more technology and resources than most individual DIY investors but the following theory of purchasing the funds are similar.

You want a globally diversified portfolio representing as many asset classes as possible using low-cost index funds. I use mostly Vanguard and DFA funds and will specifically demonstrate Vanguard funds since they are more readily available to individual investors than DFA funds.

Let's get started. First the 40% of bonds can be put in the Vanguard Total Bond Market Index Fund and Total International Bond Index Fund period. I would suggest 25%/15% respectively.

If you would prefer a deeper dive, you could put 10-15% of the money in Vanguard Inflation-Protected Securities Fund and the balance to the other two funds in proportion to my original suggestion. That takes care of the fixed portion of the portfolio.

Now I would allocate the remaining 60% for equities per the following:

Total Stock Market Index Fund	20%
Vanguard Small-Cap Value Index Fund	10%
Vanguard Emerging Markets Stock Index Fund	10%
Vanguard Developed Markets Index Fund	10%

Vanguard Total International
Stock Market Index Fund   10%

Before you get your panties in a bunch, I realize this decision is very subjective. My goal is to give a little heavier weighting to the U.S. S&P 500 companies not because they will perform better—although they have been doing well lately. It is because I believe we have a bias since we see the reporting of these market returns and better understand what to expect without panicking unnecessarily.

I also admit there can be other ways to skin this cat. If you are challenging and questioning the allocations, then you probably don't even need to be reading this book.

These are guidelines to safely get you started and learn the fundamentals. There is plenty of time to get more sophisticated if you choose. Fortunately, you don't have to be sophisticated. These basic strategies will put you ahead of over 90% of today's investors.

Before we finish this exercise let's discuss one more thing. Many investors as you saw in my example have most of their money and contributions in their 401(k). I would like to discuss how to manage those investments since you may not have control over the options within the plan.

First, I try to determine if the plan allows in-service distributions which allow us to roll out of the plan the money so that I can help you have more control over the selection of funds to use. You may be able to do that on your own as well.

Contact your Human Resources Representative and ask for "a list of my 401(k) investment options and the fees associated with each." You need to know your options and the costs for each choice. If the costs are not available, you can always use a website like Morningstar to get detailed information about each fund.

When your options are limited, you may not be able to duplicate the strategies I have outlined. Worst case scenario: if you find one decent stock fund and one decent bond fund to meet your overall asset allocation of like 60/40 that we used in our previous example, it's better than nothing and will work.

This is probably the only place I feel a target date fund should be used. They are not perfect, but they can be a good and easy way to implement your investment strategy when your options are limited or confusing.

Each target date fund should provide the funds asset allocation. Try to approximate your allocation to the fund closest rather than just using the date based on your age. Again, the Morningstar website can assist you if the information you receive from HR is not helpful. Look for the words index when looking for bond funds and look for S&P 500 index for the equity portion if the choices are limited.

This is another example where working with an advisor can be helpful. An advisor can look not only at the 401(k) but then make suggestions keeping in consideration the other buckets you have outside of the 401(k) to help create a better diversified portfolio overall.

So, for example if the 401(k) has a good S&P 500 fund you can pick then an advisor can fill the buckets with other funds to complete the strategy.

Bottom line: keep it simple, understandable and effective. If you save appropriately and invest simply and wisely, you will eventually reach the retirement summit.

This might be a good time to address a question I often hear. *"Why are you comfortable holding all your assets with one company?"*

The answer is simple: It is because the assets are invested in Vanguard or any number of other fund families such as DFA. They may be invested in funds of the same name and, through those, invested in the individual stocks and bonds those funds hold.

Even if Vanguard was to implode (a small possibility), the underlying investments would remain unaffected. They are separate from the fund company. Each fund family carries their own fraud insurance. They are regulated by the SEC and they do not have access to your money and therefore they can't make off with it.

This also addresses why it is inefficient to own a lot of similar funds by different names. They end up owning the same companies inside the fund and you could end up paying higher expenses just because they are different funds. Worse yet, one fund manager might be buying while the other fund manager is selling the same companies.

These activities don't make the portfolio safer or efficient, just costlier resulting in lower returns.

Don't forget, download the toolkit (including all the worksheets) for free! For your bonuses, go to: www.smartretirementmadesimple.com

PART III

FADS, FEARS, FACTS, AND OPINIONS

CHAPTER 7

TAXES

Because I have been a CPA for over 30 years, I focus a lot on taxes. This is one area of great value to an investor. Most investors misunderstand taxes so let's do a deep dive first with what tax brackets really mean.

There are all kinds of taxes and believe me, most of us feel we all pay our fair share. However, let's talk about federal income taxes.

They are a very progressive income tax. Currently a little bit over 40% pay nothing in federal Income tax or even get money back meaning they have a negative tax due to refundable tax credits.

The top 10% of earners pay about 70% of taxes and the top 1% of earners pay 39% of taxes. As you earn more money, not only will you pay more money, but you will pay a higher percentage of your money. Tax brackets help you comprehend your marginal tax rate. You need to understand the difference between your marginal tax rate and your effective tax rate.

The marginal tax rate is the rate at which you pay taxes on the next dollar you earn. So, if you earn another $100 and $43 goes to the tax man you are paying 43%. The other tax rate is the effective tax rate. You arrive at this percentage by taking all the taxes you pay and divide by the dollars you made.

The effective tax rate due to the progressive nature of the tax code is always less than the marginal tax rate. You might find your marginal tax rate to be 43% but your effective tax rate to be only 19%.

If you look at current tax brackets you will see that only the dollars filling up each bucket is taxed at that bucket's rate. Everybody pays at the same rate. Some people fill up more buckets resulting in more dollars being paid at the higher bracket rates for the respective buckets.

Standard deductions are different for married and single individuals but play an important part in this discussion. Income up to the standard deduction is tax-free. This strategy can be used when determining where to pull money from when taking withdrawals.

This is an important point since the tax code changed and increased the standard deduction eliminating itemizing for most taxpayers. This portion functions as a zero percent tax bracket.

Keep in mind when you move into a higher tax bracket only the dollar above the previous bracket is taxed at the higher rate. Tax breaks are not all equal. It is important to understand the difference between a **tax deduction** and a *tax credit*. A tax deduction is money you don't pay taxes on. For example, if you give $2,000 to a charity, you won't owe taxes on that $2,000 of income (a $500 savings if your marginal tax rate is 25%).

A tax credit is money paid toward your tax bill. So, a $2,000 tax credit is directly subtracted from your tax bill. Credits are better than deductions. However, remember that even two deductions in the same category can be dramatically different in size. You must love the tax code.

Just remember it never makes sense to spend $1.00 to save thirty-three cents. You will go broke and never build wealth with that philosophy. However, if you truly need to buy something anyway making the purchase tax deductible is a good decision.

One other important tax point is the difference between taxes paid and withholdings. You may be required to pay estimated taxes even if you did not take any withdrawals. You can have withholdings from earnings if you are still working but you need to be aware that the government expects you to pay taxes throughout the year as money is earned. Unfortunately, the IRS will assess penalties if you have underestimated your taxes.

Be sure to look closely if you are required to make estimates. There is no incentive to pay more than required since the government does not pay you interest but it is important to understand the rules.

Here are a few items related to taxes to follow:

- Don't spend money you otherwise would not just to get a tax deduction.
- Always look for opportunities to pay for any expenses with pre-tax dollars.

- Maximizing your retirement plan contributions often provides the largest and most valuable tax deductions.
- Be aggressive when trying to reduce your tax bill. The government doesn't give you extra points for being conservative.

Many of my clients live on over six figures annually and pay zero in taxes. This book is the foundation and path to making this happen. With some time and planning, it can be possible for you, too.

Working with an advisor who has an understanding of the tax code can pay big dividends. So many situations and circumstances have a direct connection to taxes and tax planning. Good advice in this area can provide tons of value.

Almost all financial decisions have a tax impact. If the impact of taxes is not taken into consideration while making financial decisions throughout the year, you could be paying more in income taxes than you would otherwise.

It is important to see that tax planning is not a separate function from financial planning. Instead, they should be done simultaneously while making financial decisions and incorporated into your overall financial plan.

Planning for retirement taxes can improve the odds of meeting your goals and retiring sooner. Tax planning can be a key component to analyzing current and future tax liabilities, utilizing tax strategies to shift or minimize taxes throughout your lifetime and more effectively plan your current and future cash flow.

Let me pull back the curtain and give you a peek at one of many examples of tax planning with a client. No one likes to pay any more taxes than they must. I recently worked with a soon-to-be retiring couple on finding their tax equilibrium rate for retirement liquidations.

The goal was to reduce taxes by determining the optimal balancing point between accelerating income to fill up the lower tax brackets today, but still defer enough income to fill up the tax brackets in the future as well.

We need to identify certain assumptions about Social Security and pension payments, Required Minimum Distribution (RMD) calculations, anticipated interest and dividends, and capital gains. Once we identify these assumptions we can engage in various strategies.

The ideal tax bracket to fill up will vary individual by individual but our first goal is to remain in the 12% ordinary income tax bracket (and 0% capital gains rate). Certainly, at a minimum to stay below the 24% bracket for higher income earners.

Example: Jack and Diane are both 62, getting ready to retire, and have accumulated nearly $1.3M in savings for retirement, including $400,000 in a taxable account, $700,000 in a traditional rollover IRA, and $200,000 in a ROTH IRA.

Between the two of them they are eligible for nearly $34,000/year in Social Security benefits if they start now (62) but have decided to wait until age 70 when their benefit will be increased to almost $64,000/year (plus cost-of-living adjustments). Diane will also receive a pension of nearly $20,000/year (no inflation COLA).

The couple's goal is to spend $8,000/month in retirement ($96,000/year) which will be closely covered by Diane's pension and their Social Security. The couple came to me with a plan and wanted to discuss possible other options feeling they might be missing something.

The couple's initial plan was to draw $50,000/year from their taxable account for the next eight years (largely depleting it) and supplement with $25,000/ year from their ROTH IRA (depleting this account as well).

They would be required to pay tax on qualifying interest, dividends, and capital gains but essentially no tax liability for the next eight years.

My immediate concern was their plan may be a little too tax efficient in those early eight years. I reminded them of a few landmines we needed to sniff out. Once they turn 70, their Social Security payments of nearly $80,000/year (adjusted for inflation by then and 85% taxable) will begin on top of their RMDs at age 72 that by then will be projected to be $50,000/year which alone provides more than enough cash flow to support their spending at that time.

I brought to their attention that with the standard deduction of $24,800 in 2020, they would have been eligible for the lowest 12% tax bracket on most of their income from age 62 to 70, including 0% on long-term capital gains and qualifying dividends...and then when their Social Security hits and RMDs two years later, they're pushed into the 24% bracket from which they potentially will never leave.

Normally the rule of thumb is to spend taxable accounts first and let the pre-tax accounts continue to grow tax-free. As you can see this is not always optimal and for Jack and Diane, I recommended a different option that allowed us to fill up the lower tax buckets with IRA money.

Additionally, I recommended doing partial ROTH IRA conversions of $60,000/year for the next eight to ten years, keeping them within the 12% tax bracket and whittling down their IRA before RMDs (age 72) and Social Security (age 70) begin.

The net results of finding Jack and Diane's tax equilibrium are significant: they save 12% tax rate difference (between the 24% future and 12% current tax brackets) on most of their $700,000 IRA (plus growth) withdrawals for the rest of their lives as those withdrawals occur over time, saving literally $10s of thousands of dollars in cumulative taxes over their lifetime.

The bottom line, though, is simply to understand the importance of tax planning as part of your retirement and financial planning. I experience similar experiences with practically every client.

CHAPTER 8

HSAs

Many people are not familiar with the HSA option. An HSA is a special type of account that is only available to people with a qualifying high-deductible health insurance plan.

You will recall I mentioned an HSA bucket in the waterfall strategy. An even smaller percentage of people eligible participate. For 2020, that means a health insurance plan with a deductible of at least $2,800 for families or $1,400 for individuals.

The HSA is meant to help with the cost of medical expenses, and provides excellent tax breaks to do so:

- Contributions are tax deductible
- The money grows tax-free while inside the account

- The money can be withdrawn tax-free for eligible medical expenses which have become quite broad

But there are a few more characteristics I recommend that also makes it a fantastic place to incorporate into the waterfall contributions we discussed in Part II.

The money is 100% yours and rolls over year-to-year, even if you haven't used it. This contrasts with a flex-plan where unused money is forfeited at the end of the year. The best part I like is you can invest the HSA money just like you would inside an IRA or 401(k) if you choose the right provider. While there is typically a 20% penalty in addition to taxes on any withdrawals that are not used for medical expenses, that penalty goes away once you reach 65.

I recommend paying your current medical expenses out-of-pocket. You can use the HSA as a long-term retirement planning tool. **In fact, it can be even better than an IRA or 401(k) because it's the ONLY account that offers a triple tax break: deduction on the way in, tax-free growth inside account, and tax-free withdrawals for medical expenses.**

When we get older, medical expenses are one of the uncertainties we face but it is a pretty safe bet we will incur. The ability to pay those expenses from an account tax free is an attractive option. So, if you have the option available to you, an HSA is a useful place to put some of your retirement financial savings.

One of the downsides of the HSA is that they can be a little confusing trying to figure out where to open one. It's something you must do on your own. The key for me is to have the option to invest the money in high-quality, low-cost index funds, which we've talked about through this book.

Here is a list of a few companies to check out:

- Alliant Credit Union
- HSA Bank
- Saturna Capital

Each of these companies are good options and will serve you well. But they each have different fee structures and one of them may save you more than others depending on how you plan to use it.

You should do some research to see if one stands out for your specific situation. Another resource for more research is a tool available at: *http://www.hsasearch.com/* If you are eligible to open an HSA, it can be a powerful way to save for financial independence.

Health insurance is just one part of protecting your assets. In the next chapter, we are going to cover other types of insurance policies you may consider as you develop your retirement plan.

CHAPTER 9

INSURANCE

Insurance is an important topic but can be overwhelming and beyond the scope of this book. However, due to its importance I want to cover some important and helpful areas around this topic.

Mortality, disability, and morbidity (specifically the need for long-term care and even longevity risk—living longer than expected) are all risks important to address. You can have the best investment plan going and if these areas are not addressed your plan can implode.

The largest asset for many families is labor capital—the present value of future earned income streams. Without that asset, or insurance to protect against the loss of that asset, you may not be able to maintain an acceptable standard of living for your family.

A critical part of the financial planning process is analyzing the need for life, health, long-term care, disability, and all types of what are referred to as "personal lines" of insurance. All existing policies should be reviewed often. Policies should also be reviewed after life events such as a birth, death, divorce or other significant changes.

Insurance is not exciting but can be vital to protect us against worst-case scenarios. I want to briefly touch on some insurance areas of particular importance.

You buy life insurance because you love someone else, and you care about their well-being. In order to provide for all the things a family will need if the income disappears the obvious question becomes "how much coverage is needed and for how long?"

There are two main types of life insurance: term and permanent. Many use the term "whole life" to describe any type of permanent coverage. The least expensive way to provide the most significant coverage is through term insurance.

Term insurance can provide a level premium for a specified amount of time, which is typically 10, 15, 20, 25, or 30 years. They usually also have a conversion feature to a permanent policy without providing evidence of insurability in case that option becomes necessary.

Permanent insurance tends to be complex and normally the complexity favors the insurance company. I tend to only favor permanent insurance to provide liquidity for an estate that will be subject to the federal estate tax.

Choosing only from among the highest rated insurers is critical (only AAA- and-AA rated). **Never allow a permanent insurance policy to be on autopilot.** Regular reviews on these complicated products are a must.

One other potential benefit of a permanent insurance plan is the long-term care benefit rider that can be available. Be cautious and make sure you understand how these work and evaluate the costs for such benefits. Traditional long-term care and disability insurance can be important and should be explored. However, these topics are beyond the scope of this book.

My goal here is to encourage you to determine where these topics fit in with your overall financial plan. Seek professional help and even look for options with your employer if you are still working.

Personal lines of insurance are again beyond the scope of this book, but I want to mention a few areas you should understand that can play an important role in the management of risk. You should at least review annually the following examples:

Homeowners insurance: It is critical to have proper flood, hurricane or earthquake coverage. Make sure renovations have been updated and valuable possessions are covered. Some things may require a separate line of coverage.

Auto insurance: It should always cover insured and uninsured motorists so that an accident will always be covered.

Policy Liability Limits: Make sure your automobile and homeowners (renters) insurance policy liability limits are several hundred thousand dollars.

Umbrella insurance: This type of policy provides excess coverage above your traditional homeowners and auto insurance. It is probably the most underutilized type of coverage. It is relatively inexpensive but can provide protection against major claims or lawsuits.

A good example would be if someone slips on your sidewalk during a winter snow and sues you for not properly cleaning and salting the walk. Don't be foolish to think this can't happen to you.

I recommend you carry a $1 million to $5 million umbrella policy above and beyond your auto and homeowner's policy limits.

Insurance is one of those areas that you are hoping for the best but planning for the worst. You purchase insurance hoping to never have a claim and later consider it to be a waste of money. However, if needed, it can keep a good financial plan on track.

One last point on insurance. Never mix insurance with investing. Insurance is for protection not investments.

FIVE MUST-HAVE INSURANCE POLICIES

Just because some aspects of money are not talked about much, doesn't mean it's not important. I am not suggesting you always need all five, just that stuff like this can get away from you and can turn bad quickly over time. Things change and you should periodically review these areas.

LIFE INSURANCE

If you die with no life insurance, your family could be stuck in a dire situation forcing drastic changes, all while grieving you. If you pass on, your family likely may need to replace your income.

This is the major reason to need life insurance and I can help you determine if you need the insurance and how much.

LONG-TERM DISABILITY INSURANCE

If you are permanently disabled, you will be unable to produce an income and yet still need to be cared for. Disability insurance can potentially provide say 70% of your income, usually until death or at least age 65.

Often the cheapest place to acquire this insurance is through your employment. The older you get the more expensive and difficult to acquire.

LONG-TERM CARE INSURANCE

This really isn't necessary until you hit age 60. After that it becomes a little more vital if you can afford this. If you wait too long after 60 it becomes less affordable.

The main question is who's going to take care of you if the need arises. Educate yourself on the costs and discuss with your spouse and family the plan in the event something happens.

HOMEOWNERS/RENTER'S INSURANCE

You should never own or rent property without having yourself covered in the case of a fire, flood, burglary or some other disaster. Renter's insurance is relatively cheap to get. When buying homeowners insurance, get one that has guaranteed replacement costs.

Try to maintain an emergency fund in place so you can take lower premiums and higher deductibles.

UMBRELLA POLICY

Consider an umbrella insurance policy rider on your homeowner's insurance for extra liability protection. This insurance is inexpensive and can create protection against the litigious society we live in today. If you have worked hard to build up some assets, this is a good way to add an extra layer of protection for a very reasonable cost.

Reviewing your insurance policies can add protection but also save you money by cancelling once you reach a point in life you no longer need them or maybe not need as much.

Insurance gets very expensive as we get older. It should always be updated as part of our overall financial plan. Next, we will review social security. It was deducted from your employment years. What happens when you reach retirement age? Let's find out.

CHAPTER 10

SOCIAL SECURITY

All my financial planning in the past has been based on not receiving Social Security. I now take the position that it is too popular and would be political suicide to abandon.

I do however believe how it is paid and taxed will likely change. Based on what we have paid in—and assuming we live long enough—could provide a hefty amount to subsidize our retirement.

The huge baby boomer generation has started collecting Social Security benefits and living longer while the contributions from them have declined or stopped. You need to really crunch the numbers and know some important rules before deciding to collect Social Security.

Once you reach age 62, you can begin collecting Social Security. The catch is the sooner you start, the smaller your checks. The flip side though, is the longer you delay, the fewer years you'll be collecting. This is where crunching the numbers will help you decide **when** to collect it.

The subject of Social Security can be a whole book in itself and many exist. I just want to whet your appetite and hit the high points. Getting some professional help and guidance can be invaluable.

The biggest consideration is when do you need the money? Not "want" the money but truly need the money. If you need it now, then nothing else really matters.

If you need to continue working during the years of 62 until your full retirement age of likely 66 and months (depending on your birth date) you need to be aware of a severe penalty for collecting Social Security during this period. If you earn more than $18,960 annually your benefits will be reduced by $1 for every $2 earned. This is very costly.

The longer you live, the more advantageous delaying is. The breakeven point between age 62-66 is around 84.

When the month full retirement age is reached, there is no limit on earnings related to a penalty. However, up to 85% of your Social Security still may be taxable. You also gain 8% in an annual benefit per year past your full retirement benefit age. This could be as much as a 32% increase at age 70.

There is no benefit waiting past age 70 but clearly some good planning may improve your financial picture. All options should be taken into consideration before deciding. Once decisions are made, they are difficult to impossible to reverse.

I encourage you to go to the Social Security website *http://ssa.gov/myaccount/*. Once you create an account for yourself, you'll be able to track where you stand. You'll also be able to check and make sure that the record of your earnings is accurate.

This is very important as the size of your checks will be in part determined by how much you earned over the years. Over a third of people take their benefit at 62.

Two thirds never wait until full retirement age which for most people today is around 67. Many people like the couple I mentioned early in this book have just not saved enough to meet the gap and are wholly dependent upon Social Security for their retirement.

I'm going to lay out a scenario that just might give you some hope and options if this describes your situation. These suggestions are not necessarily ideal and attractive, but they are real and should be considered.

If you are going to be solely dependent upon Social Security, you need to focus on two things. The first is to eliminate your mortgage. This one item is normally the largest expense for most people. To eliminate this expenditure, however, it is critical you pay off the mortgage or downsize before retiring.

The second critical factor is the need to work until full retirement age. This may not be attractive but if you have not planned prior to reading this book or if you are not able to fill the gap you are calculating in this book—this is your only option. Not ideal but stay with me.

One of the reasons most people don't save is they just didn't have enough discretionary money to save. The median household income in the US (2019) was $60,000. This may be you. My example though can work even if your income was higher. You will likely be needing to retire on a similar amount.

Let's assume this couple has been earning an equivalent amount of money their entire life adjusted for inflation. This means that thirty years ago they were making $30,000, which is equivalent to $60,000 today.

In reality this couple has been living on less than $60,000. In fact, after income tax, FICA, and any contributions to their retirement plans and mortgage, they are living on about $43,000. How do I get that?

Their tax burden, to include FICA is $11,205 including State income tax. That's 18.67% of their gross income. Let's say they are contributing 10% so that would be another $6,000 or so in take home pay. This is a total of approximately $17,000 from the gross of $60,000 to get us our $43,000.

There will possibly be other expenses such as mortgage related to working but let's leave those alone for now.

The calculated monthly Social Security income will be $2,137.08 or $25,644 a year. This amount replaces 59.6% of your actual net income. Not too shabby but it is about to get better.

A married couple means the spouse gets the option to collect her own benefit based on her earnings or against his/her spouses' earnings. Since the family earnings were $60,000 let's assume mom/dad stayed home with the kids. The spousal benefit would be half of the primary spouse benefit which gives us another $1,068.54 (1/2 of $2,137.08)

Add $2,137.08 and $1,068.54 to get a monthly benefit of $3,205.62 at full retirement age, $38,467 annually. That now replaces 89% of the net income pre-retirement.

A one-worker household with income of $60,000 will have a 99.35% of their net income replaced by Social Security at 69 years old since the primary wage earner will earn an additional 8% from full retirement age to age 70. If you are putting any money aside at all you're even more golden.

Clearly the same results are not possible as your income dramatically increases above the $60,000 but it sure makes that gap smaller by doing these two things related to Social Security: 1) work a little longer and 2) eliminate your highest expense, your mortgage, to get the required net income as low as possible.

If most people eliminated all their high debt on just homes, cars, vacations, and other extravagant expenses, they might be closer to the $60-80,000 net income needed to live than you think.

I hope this one chapter gives you hope and encouragement. The industry certainly doesn't want you to see this simple reality. Social Security is a very important decision to your future financial health.

Husbands particularly need to read this chapter closely, because their decisions about how long to work and when to begin claiming Social Security benefits could have substantial impact on the quality of their wives' later years.

And to be honest here, the odds favor that many of these years will be spent as widows. Decisions should be made with likely longevity in mind.

CHAPTER 11

TO ROTH OR NOT TO ROTH

There are several ways in which a traditional IRA differs from a ROTH IRA. Many books have been written explaining how they differ and the mechanics of each.

I am going to try to focus on when and how they should be used and discuss the growing benefits of doing ROTH conversions. The biggest difference between a traditional IRA and a ROTH IRA is how they are taxed. It is important to understand marginal tax rates and effective tax rates to clearly understand something many people get wrong about Traditional IRA's and ROTH IRA's.

Conventional wisdom looks at your marginal tax rate today vs. your marginal tax rate in the future. That is wrong. Contributions to traditional IRA's will likely save you money at your marginal rate today, but withdrawals in retirement will be taxed at an effective tax rate that's quite likely to be lower.

What you need to do instead is compare your MARGINAL tax rate TODAY with your EFFECTIVE tax rate in the FUTURE.

This is true for a few reasons:

1. Tax brackets are large, spanning tens of thousands of dollars.
2. Most contributions will save you at the marginal tax bracket. The higher bracket amount unless you are already at the lowest bracket.
3. Most withdrawals in retirement will likely be larger making it likely the effective rate will be lower since you will be working through several tax brackets.

Let's look at an example:

- Two married couples each making $53,000 puts them in the 15% marginal bracket
- They each contribute $12,000 to IRAs

- Or they could contribute to their ROTH IRAs in which they could only contribute $9,350 due to 15% taxes

Conventional wisdom says that their 15% tax bracket is low and they should therefore contribute to a ROTH IRA. So how does it actually play out?

After 30 years the Traditional IRA has significantly more money than the ROTH IRA. Again, conventional wisdom claims that because they are in the 15% tax bracket both now and in retirement, they should end up with the same amount of income whichever way they contributed.

When you apply a 4.5% withdrawal rate such as I have recommended throughout this book, conventional wisdom does not play out and the traditional IRA works out to be better.

What's the reason for the difference? The big reason why the traditional IRA comes out ahead has to do with the difference between marginal and effective tax rates we just talked about.

In our example, the couple's ROTH IRA contributions would be taxed at marginal 15%, while their traditional IRA contributions would be taxed at 0% and the traditional IRAs' withdrawals would be taxed at an effective rate of 2.44%.

So, by choosing the traditional IRA, the couple would be choosing to pay 12.56% less in taxes, even though their marginal rate would be the same at each point in time. Over thirty years of saving, that adds up to a significant difference.

To be clear, this doesn't mean that a traditional IRA is always better than a ROTH IRA. There are many variables that make your specific situation different from our example. Some of those variables can tilt the scales in either direction.

Here are a few of the reasons to favor a ROTH IRA:

1. **We gave an example based upon math.** In terms of actual behavior many people will end up contributing more after-tax dollars to a ROTH IRA than a traditional IRA because the mental accounting is easier. Also, the tax savings spread out over a year on lower contributions often go

unnoticed. Maxing out the ROTH can be simpler even though not mathematically perfect.

2. **You expect to have other income in retirement.** Our example assumed your only income in addition to the IRA was Social Security. Other income starts to fill up those lower brackets leaving the IRA withdrawals being fully taxed at your marginal rate in retirement.

   The point is income in addition to IRA withdrawals can increase the effective rate. Some tax-free ROTH IRA money can avoid extra taxes.

3. **Tax diversification.** Having some money in a traditional IRA will give you the opportunity to fill up some of the lower tax brackets in retirement. This lets you save more in taxes today that you'll have to pay back later. Having money in a ROTH IRA will protect you from the risk of higher tax rates in the future. Diversification doesn't have to be 50-50.

4. **You want to pay for certainty later.** The reality is we do not know what future tax rates will be. You may want the comfort of knowing you'll be able to access tax free money.

A ROTH IRA can also serve very much like a savings account. The availability of contributions, college savings, required minimum distributions not taxable slowing the tax bite vs. traditional, and estate planning all make a ROTH very attractive.

Do I have your head swimming? Let's keep going. Keep in mind that if you have already been contributing to IRAs in the past there are still many opportunities. There can be many reasons why you might be in a lower tax bracket in the future creating opportunities to take advantage of ROTH conversions.

These opportunities allow you to win at the beginning when making contributions and win on the back end making conversions. The potential to avoid or reduce state income tax in retirement can become attractive for conversions.

Lastly, there are many tax credits and deductions that can be beneficial to make IRA contributions rather than ROTH contributions because traditional IRA contributions reduce AGI which many credits and deductions are based on.

Conversion options give you flexibility and choices. Fortunately, there are no income limits or limits to the amounts you convert. You just need to crunch the numbers. If you're contributing to one of them, you're in good shape. The general rule is that you convert up to the top of a certain tax bracket. That might be the 12% bracket or perhaps even the 22% bracket in 2020.

Generally doing conversions above this amount isn't advised unless you expect a great deal of taxable income in retirement. The other key ingredient is you should have taxable money to pay the tax. Do not pay the tax from the IRA money. This just triggers additional tax on the conversion creating an endless cycle. The ability to pay the tax with after-tax money also plays hard into the decision to convert and how much.

I hope I have challenged you to crunch the numbers and explore the opportunities a ROTH IRA may provide. Each situation can be unique and will require some digging to figure out the right answer.

CHAPTER 12

DEBT

The acceptance of debt is the single biggest reason people will not become wealthy and be in control of their financial destiny.

Some people struggle with how much they should spend on a home. I suggest two guidelines. The first is to never carry a mortgage larger than twice your gross income. The second is to spend less than 20% of your gross income on housing, including your mortgage.

Although I don't consider a home an investment, one could evaluate the purchase of a home from the point of view of an investor. For example, if you can rent a similar home for $2,000 per month but you must spend $600,000 to purchase it, that means it has a cap rate of only = $2,000 x 12 months x 55%/ $600,000 = 2.2%. You are almost surely better off renting that home rather than purchasing. On the other hand, if the home will sell for $400,000 and rent for $4,000 per month, then your cap rate is 6.6%, which is quite good.

Speaking of homes. If you are married and your state allows for "Tenants by the Entirety," be sure to use it. This means that both husband and wife own 100% of the home. So, a successful lawsuit that only names the husband cannot take the home, because the wife owns 100% of it and vice versa.

HOW DO I GET MY DEBT UNDER CONTROL?

Here's what I'd do: Make a list of all debts. Eliminate all non-essential spending, and I mean all of it. Those routine $5 coffees, $20 dinners, and $12 cocktails add up. This is what will free up the money you need to extinguish the debt flames that burn up your life and keep you from true investing.

You need to eliminate all your personal and consumer debt, particularly high interest debt before you shift major money to investments. Spend less than you earn. Invest the surplus. Avoid debt. Refer to the waterfall plan and you will see where to emphasize debt reduction.

I want to give you another example that may not help you if you are planning to retire in the next ten years — but it can't hurt and might be something to pass on to your children or grandchildren.

The decision I am talking about is buying a car that is 5 years old versus a new car. Statistics show that the annual difference in cost is around $6,000 for this simple decision. Investing this extra $6,000 per year would give you $80,000 in ten years and a whopping $500,000 in thirty years. This is your future financial health that debt destroys.

You have noticed I haven't even discussed credit cards since I'm sure you know the danger of not paying your card off each and every month. Debt is the enemy. **Start sacrificing today so you can live like nobody else later.**

CHAPTER 13

EXTRA INGREDIENTS

To suggest the strategies and principles I am about to discuss as advanced might be a bit of a stretch. You can accomplish retirement bliss as simply as we have previously discussed.

I share the following subjects mainly because most investors hear about them from the industry and may want to understand them better at some point. After you have conquered the basics, you may want to implement a few into your plan of action.

ANNUITIES

Annuities are the least understood investment option. There are so many variations and the insurance industry has a vested interest in making them as complex as possible. They break two of my golden rules: 1) If it is too difficult to understand, avoid them and 2) avoid anything if it looks and sounds too good to be true.

With that said I do believe there is one annuity that might be useful in specific circumstances. This annuity would be an immediate annuity.

These annuities start shortly after a contract is signed. These annuities are more for very conservative investors and folks that have legitimate fear and concern of running out of money. In other words, they read this book way too late.

Deferred annuities which are predominantly what the industry is peddling mostly to older Americans, are just not normally appropriate. Variable annuities and equity indexed annuities are the most common. These products generate big fat commissions.

Agents tout these annuities telling prospects they will not have to pay any tax on the money inside the annuity until it's pulled out. Here is the part they leave out: when you withdraw the money, you'll owe ordinary income taxes on the gains in the annuity. Also, you will be subject to a 10 percent IRS penalty if you withdraw the money before age fifty-nine and a half.

If you would have stuffed that money in a tax efficient taxable account instead, the profits would have been taxed at the favorable long-term capital gains rate. This feature haunts your heirs more if the money ends up being passed to them since they will be responsible for paying all the tax—leaving them with less money.

The equity indexed annuity is even more confusing because they appear to deliver on the promise of having your cake and eat it too. The salespeople selling these products are not constrained by the federal securities regulation's investment advisors must obey. Just do an online search for "equity indexed annuities." You will see a whole host of lawsuits over their use and abuse.

Annuities are basically insurance products, and I don't consider them to be investments. The story most investors are told is that during good times, the equity-indexed-annuity provides an investor with a portion of the market's return.

Depending on the contract it could be varying percentages of the return but not 100%. During bad times, the equity-indexed-annuity will protect you by providing a guaranteed return, such as 3% or even just protection of never going below 0%.

This is the point: things get complex. Frankly, even many agents don't understand the details such as the provider can legally lower your returns. The returns could be less than a U.S. Treasury Bill. It's also hard to ditch these products creating a liquidity concern due to surrender periods that can last as long as ten years or more causing you to forfeit 10 to 12 percent of your money.

The motivation for selling these products is the prospect of capturing large commissions. This creates a huge conflict of interest. An advisor is often tempted to push a $250,000 sale that would give him a commission of $20,000 versus managing the account for $2,500. Equity-indexed-annuities are unsuitable investments.

SEQUENCE OF RETURNS

The sequence of returns risk is probably the biggest risk facing recent retirees. This risk occurs when markets decline in the first few years of retirement, depleting the portfolio in large amounts while taking distributions and not having enough time to recover before you run out of money.

Unfortunately, a lot of agents and even advisors introduce equity-indexed-annuities to the picture—touting guarantees against such results. Read the section on annuities for some additional color to this subject.

There are several ways to manage the sequence of return risk while maintaining the equity portfolio I recommend throughout this book.

My solution to the potential problem resulting from a sequence of return disaster in the first years of retirement is what I call the bucket cushion. This essentially is a reserve fund held in a special bucket to avoid portfolio withdrawals from your primary buckets during down years.

When the down years hit, you just turn off the regular withdrawal bucket and start drawing from the reserve bucket. The question is what amount of cash should be in this bucket? I suggest the following calculation:

Reserve Bucket = Annual Spending − (portfolio x Annual Yield) x # Years

I recommend using an average yield of 2.5% and calculate for three years. I use a yield number because even though the market may be down the reserve bucket portfolio, I recommend it has a yield since a good portion is made up of ETF's.

These spin off distributions each month, and for a predominantly bond-allocated bucket, the yield would average 2.5%. The median length of down markets is two years so this makes me comfortable.

An example from our couple with a $1M portfolio and a spending requirement from the portfolio of $45,000 (4.5% x $1M) would equal $60,000.

Plug the numbers in to the calculation:

Reserve Bucket = $45,000 − ($1M x 2.5%) x Reserve Bucket = $60,000

This amount would fund our reserve bucket to be released during down markets in those early years. This amount is significantly less than holding three years in cash. If you have a large enough portfolio to create that much safety, knock yourself out.

You may need to keep more of that money working if things are a little tighter. This is a method to accomplish the task and still protect you from running out of money.

Once you get through a few years of retirement you should have built up enough of a cushion that it will no longer matter.

SAVINGS RATE VS. RETURN RATE

This topic may very well be one of the most important you may read in this book. The subject is important for early or beginner savers and particularly for late savers trying to catch up in the next ten years.

Many investors focus on increasing or "chasing" higher returns in the market. Both have a place, but your savings rate is more important. The rate of return becomes more important after you have built up wealth.

There are people in the world making 10% less than you who are not ragged and homeless. Live like them.

Remember, it's not how much money you make, it's how much money you keep. To build wealth, there's only one path forward: sheer brute savings.

Let's take two identical people. Tom and Jerry. Both are 50 and both are late to the savings game and are motivated to get back on track in the next ten years. Both make $150,000 per year.

Tom could consistently get 12% for ten full years. Tom will have $235,855 in 10 years saving 8% ($12,000/$150,000).

Jerry focuses on maximizing his savings rate. He can put away $2,000 a month but only gets half of Tom's return but still a healthy 6% return in the market using the methods described throughout this book. Jerry will have $335,319 in ten years.

If he increases his savings rate to $3,000 a month, in ten years he will have $502,979. This is accomplished with a savings rate of 16% and 24% respectively.

The facts are that it takes about 11 years for investment returns to account for more annual net worth growth than savings. When you are just starting your investment journey or trying to catch up in ten years you just can't accomplish the goal with return focus only.

In the long run, no one can deny that compound interest is a powerful force. But in the short run, the savings rate is far more powerful.

For anyone just starting or wanting to catch up in ten years or less, your focus should be on your savings rate more than your returns.

Your savings rate number is the number one factor of how soon you will reach the higher balance required to meet your goal.

Meeting long-term financial goals and independence generally requires investing., because investing is the most efficient way to grow your money over many years.

The truth is that while there are a million things you could worry about accomplishing this feat, there's only one thing that really matters. And the good news is that it's one thing you're in complete control over:

YOUR SAVINGS RATE..................The Power of SAVING.

Let me help show another powerful exercise with a visual.

Let's compare two people, Jack and Jill. Both of them make $75,000.00 per year and are ready to start saving in their SIMPLE plan, but they go about it in different ways.

Jack frees up enough money to save 5% of his income. He is lucky enough to live through a good market and earns a 10% annual return which is pretty good.

Jill decides to not invest her money in the market and basically earns a big fat 0% return. Maybe not the best move in the world, but she also finds enough room in her budget to save 10% of her income.

So, we have Jack, saving 5% of his income and earning 10% returns.

And we have Jill, saving 10% of her income and earning 0% returns.

Who does better? Here's the chart:

YEAR	JACK	JILL	ANNUAL INCOME
\multicolumn{4}{c}{SAVINGS RATE VS. RATE of RETURN}			
0	$3,750.00	$7,500.00	$75,000
1	$7,875.00	$15,000.00	
2	$12,413.00	$22,500.00	
3	$17,404.00	$30,000.00	Jack
4	$22,894.00	$37,500.00	Savings Rate 5%
5	$28,934.00	$45,000.00	Rate of Return 10%
6	$35,577.00	$52,500.00	
7	$42,885.00	$60,000.00	
8	$50,923.00	$67,500.00	Jill
9	$59,765.00	$75,000.00	Savings Rate 10%
10	$69,492.00	$82,500.00	Rate of Return 0%
11	$80,191.00	$90,000.00	
12	$91,960.00	$97,500.00	14 YEARS
13	$104,906.00	$105,000.00	
14	$119,147.00	$112,500.00	

Remember Jack is earning 10% returns every year. Jill is earning nothing. And it still takes 14 years !!! before Jack's incredible returns are able to overcome Jill's savings rate.

That is the power of the savings rate

The higher your savings rate, the quicker your path to achieving your financial goals. Even just a 5% increase in your savings rate can knock more than a decade off your working years.

THE MORAL OF THE STORY

Eventually, the returns you earn start to matter a lot more. After the fourteenth year, Jack's balance starts growing significantly faster than Jill's because he's earning a much higher rate and taking advantage of the compounding.

What matters most is you start saving enough now so that your account balance is eventually big enough for those returns to have an impact.

In other words, you don't have to put a lot of pressure on yourself to make the right investment decisions right from the beginning. Mistakes are OK, because the return you earn, good or bad, doesn't have much impact anyways.

BUT you do need to do two things now:

1. Start saving now with whatever you can handle and

2. Put most of your energy into increasing your savings rate wherever it needs to be, not on choosing the "perfect" investments. I recommend targeting at least 15% and maybe even higher if you are older and getting a late start.

Once you have increased or maxed your savings rate, here are three things you might consider increasing your return rate.

First, invest in funds with low cost and expense ratios. Actively managed funds have higher expenses to which many are hidden. Second, increase your equity allocation a mere 10%. And third, add equity asset classes such as US Small Cap stocks, US Large Cap Value and US Small Cap Value stocks.

TAX LOSS HARVESTING

Tax-loss harvesting is all the rage these days. So, what is tax-loss harvesting?

You are allowed to deduct up to $3,000 per year of a short or long-term capital loss from your ordinary income on your taxes. Losses also offset gains.

Unfortunately, taxable losses usually show up after an investment goes down in value, not exactly the best time to sell an investment. Buying high and selling low is a losing proposition most of the time.

Most people are in a lower tax bracket, meaning capital gains offers no benefit to tax loss harvest. I also prefer to use tax efficient funds and place any funds that might tempt me to use this strategy in their appropriate buckets. Also, unless you are holding individual stocks you can normally accomplish similar results through rebalancing.

The bottom line is tax-loss harvesting can prove useful in certain circumstances but can be overly complicated and result in some very negative results.

If not properly exercised. You run the risk of falling victim to wash sale rules and the 60-day dividend rule. The fact you often are just deferring taxes creates too many opportunities for bad behavior.

This is a strategy best to work with an advisor if you feel the itch to venture down this path.

DOLLAR COST AVERAGING

Most investors build their fortunes month by month through paycheck by paycheck. This method will always buy fewer shares as market prices rise and more shares as they fall. This proves helpful since human nature causes most people to do the opposite if given a choice.

Since equity market returns are positive more than seventy percent of the time, dollar cost averaging is not, other than behaviorally, necessarily a big deal long-term. This raises the question on the benefits of dollar cost averaging lump sums. Most often averaging lump sums over any meaningful intervals will most often lead to higher average costs (and therefore lower average returns) than investing it all as soon as possible.

With dollar cost averaging, you are betting the market will drop, saving yourself some pain. You are basically saying the market is too high to invest all at once.

You have strayed into the murky world of market timing. This is another loser's game.

Let me be clear, I strongly recommend investing lump sums immediately. However, emotions should always be considered and each of the scenarios of standard systematic investing and lump sum investing should be two separate and distinct decisions.

WHAT ABOUT ALTERNATIVES?

We often hear about non-traditional investments like private equity funds, hedge funds, commodities, crypto currency, and gold.

The common argument is they are diversifiers or provide an inflation hedge and produce good returns. Unfortunately, these strategies expose us to unnecessary risks that we really don't understand.

The increased risk is normally due to using large amounts of borrowed money, making concentrated bets, trading excessively, and relying on subjective forecasts. Exclusivity can sometimes create an aura of mystery and attraction. But just because something is hard to get does not mean it is a good investment, appropriate, or necessary to achieve financial freedom.

Additionally, many alternative investments are higher in cost, less diversified, more leveraged, and less liquid than traditional investments like mutual funds.

The biggest problem with alternatives like crypto currency and gold is they do not generate any earnings, pay interest, or create business value. They are always a speculative bet in which there is a winner and loser at the end of the trade.

Frankly, a broad-based stock mutual fund portfolio already has significant commodity exposure through ownership of companies involved in these type industries. Gold is a very popular and often discussed alternative investment. I remember 1980 like yesterday since that is the year I graduated from high school.

I remember working a summer job at a local hotel where the gold buyers were busy dealing with lines of people selling jewelry when it was a record high of $850. On March 19, 2002, gold was trading at $293, well below the twenty years ago high. The inflation rate for the same period was 3.9 percent. Thus, gold's loss in purchasing power, the true inflation hedge measure, was down about 85 percent. How can this be an inflation hedge?

My belief is that you don't need alternative investments in your portfolio to have a successful investment experience, particularly considering the higher costs and liquidity constraints.

You have learned throughout this book that you likely will not have the extra discretionary money to make these types of investments if you prioritize your efforts and follow a prudent investment plan.

ACTIVE VS. PASSIVE

Active investing simply means the money managers are attempting to "beat the market" using techniques such as stock picking, market timing and track record investing. In contrast, passive money managers avoid forecasts and take a longer-term view, working to deliver market-like returns whatever they may be.

I ascribe to "The Efficient Markets Hypothesis" which asserts that no investor can beat the market over long periods except by chance. The preponderance of evidence and data shows that the efforts of active managers are unsuccessful outperforming the passive money managers.

The more sensible approach to investing would be passive investing in my opinion. This is based on the belief that markets are efficient and extremely difficult to beat, especially after costs.

The best method of investing is called indexing, which involves purchasing all the securities in a benchmark index in the exact proportions as the index. The most popular benchmark index is the S&P 500.

The biggest problem with active management is money managers tend to hold more cash looking for the next winner and they tend to abandon true diversification by overlapping their holdings to try and satisfy investors and end up drifting away from the desired asset allocation.

Most investors are not even aware these things are happening to their portfolio since they often do not participate in the decisions to buy and sell. Despite the inefficiencies created by these actions, the increased costs from active management becomes the biggest reason to avoid active management.

These higher costs break down into three categories. First, higher manager expenses tend to be higher by at least one percent due to marketing, sales costs, fees, loads and research analysis. Second, the turnover of the funds in the portfolio are higher resulting in higher commissions and fees that are passed on to the investor and create lower returns. It is not uncommon for active funds to exceed passive funds in turnover ratio by as much as four times. Finally, the third category is that you have greater tax exposure because of the increased trading.

Many investors never see these expenses. Only manager expenses are disclosed to investors. An investor can look up funds using a service like Morningstar and compare these costs for themselves. Some major custodians and brokerage firms tout "no fees," which is misleading when they don't disclose these "hidden" type fees. There are no free lunches.

In conclusion I would never suggest you can't meet your goals using active money management. I just believe passive is a simpler and less risky way to accomplish the goal.

STRUCTURED INDEX FUNDS VS LOW-COST RETAIL INDEX FUNDS?

I follow three principles to build portfolios using index funds. Index funds are preferred to actively managed funds for these three reasons. First, they provide adequate diversification, second academic engineering, and third adequate discipline.

Keep in mind though that because of these three reasons all index funds are not alike.

Here are my 12 reasons why I use my selected index funds rather than regular low-cost retail index funds:

1. You won't have to deal with pushy salesmen or brokers.
2. With an index fund, you know exactly what you're getting.
3. You don't have to fall in and out of love with individual stocks.
4. Your expenses will be the lowest of all funds.
5. Your capital gains taxes will likely be lower.
6. What goes on inside the fund is simple and transparent.
7. Index funds are boring.
8. Index funds lower portfolio turnover.

9. Index funds keep your money working for you. Not idle in cash.
10. Investors worry about losing all their money, with Index Funds there's virtually no chance.
11. Index funds are amongst the easiest of all investments to understand.
12. Index funds are managed with strict regulations, minimizing risk.

Using index funds creates a sleep-easy investment. They're highly regulated, cost very little to buy and own, and they give you massive diversification that's easy to understand and control. They're very liquid and require little emotional involvement. They also are recommended by the most trustworthy people in the industry.

I believe almost all investors can get what they need from properly engineered portfolios using index funds. They provide respectable returns and are likely to continue doing so.

PART IV

NEXT STEPS

CHAPTER 14

WHAT IS THE BEST WAY TO SPEND MONEY AND TIME?

One of the best parts of my job is getting to tell couples that they can afford to spend more money. Hopefully, you have learned a few things here that will give you the positive outcome of learning, saving, and investing over a lifetime of work.

Keep in mind I am not suggesting acquiring more things, but rather increasing your happiness quotient by spending money on **experiences**. We remember experiences long afterward, while we soon become accustomed to our possessions.

Several years ago, while our adult children were beginning to build their own lives by adding spouses and our hope for grandchildren, we determined deep in our heart that the lasting memories of family time, the reinforced network of extended family relationships, and the sense of "clan" are worth so much more than anything money could buy now or later.

We also knew that as our kids' families grew it would get harder and more difficult to pull things off if we didn't start some kind of tradition worth keeping.

We spend four days to a week each year and I pick up the tab for the entire group. Yes, it can get expensive but my... how we have all grown close. As our family expands with the addition of our grandkids, what wonderful memories we are creating.

My bucket list includes planning a trip to Disney's Magic Kingdom. My parents were snowbirds spending over 18 years in Orlando and my kids remember making many trips to visit and enjoy the Disney experience. I can't wait to see those happy faces again making a multi-generational experience something money really can't buy. Now that is true wealth.

I can only hope I have started a legacy that will continue through future generations. I consider this a wise investment. You may want to follow this lesson too.

To put this into perspective, I will share the following story:

Once upon a time an investment banker was at a pier of a small coastal Mexican village when a small boat with just one fisherman docked. Inside the small boat were several large yellowfin tunas. The American complimented the Mexican on the quality of his fish and asked how long it took him to catch them.

The Mexican replied, "only a little while."

The American then asked why didn't he stay out longer to catch more fish?

The Mexican said he had enough to support his family's immediate needs.

The American then asked, "but what do you do with the rest of your time?"

The Mexican fisherman said, "I sleep late, fish a little, play with my children, take siestas with my wife, Maria, and stroll into the village each evening where I sip wine, and play guitar with my amigos. I have a full and busy life."

The American scoffed. "I have an MBA from Harvard, and can help you," he said. "You should spend more time fishing, and the proceeds, buy a bigger boat. With the proceeds from the bigger boat, you could buy several boats, and eventually you would have a fleet of fishing boats.

Instead of selling your catch to a middleman, you could sell directly to the processor, eventually opening your own cannery. You could control your product, processing, and distribution." He spoke. "Of course, you would need to leave this small coastal village and move to Mexico City, then Los Angeles, and eventually to New York City, where you will run your expanding enterprise."

The Mexican fisherman asked, "But, how long will this take?"

To which the American replied, "Oh, 15 to 20 years or so."

"But what then?" asked the Mexican.

The American laughed and said, "That's the best part. When the time was right, you would announce an IPO, and sell your company stock to the public and become very wealthy. You would make millions!"

"Millions – then what?"

The American said, "Then you could retire. Move to a small coastal fishing village where you can sleep late, fish a little, play with your kids, take siestas with your wife, and stroll to the village in the evenings where you could sip wine and play guitar with your amigos."

Moral of the story: **Always keep in perspective the real value of your money and time. Life is a journey not a destination.**

CHAPTER 15

SHOULD YOU HIRE A FINANCIAL ADVISOR?

Whether we are talking about home repairs or investing, most people fall into two categories: those who hire professionals and the do-it-yourselfers. Sometimes the damage done by financial errors can take years to recover from—often they are irreversible. I have tried to give you solid foundational principles to avoid these mistakes.

Remember, an advisor is to help establish and quantify goals, make a plan, and fund a portfolio with the optimal historical probability of achieving your goals. He/She cannot help you do what you are now doing, any better than you are doing now. No one can.

Here are some questions to ask yourself and consider:

- Am I confident I have all the knowledge needed to develop an investment plan, integrate it into a holistic estate, tax and risk management plan and then provide the ongoing care and maintenance that is required?
- Do I have the mathematical skills required? You need more than basic math skills. You need to understand advanced probability theory and statistics, such as correlations.
- Do I have the ability to determine the appropriate asset allocation, one that provides the greatest odds of achieving my financial goals while not taking more risk than I have the ability and willingness to take?
- Do I have strong knowledge of financial history? You should know things such as how often stocks provided negative returns, how long bear markets last, and how deep bear markets have been. Otherwise, you will repeat past mistakes.
- Do I have the temperament and emotional discipline needed to stick with a plan in the face of many potential crises I will almost certainly experience. Will I be able to avoid panicking? Will I be OK with rebalancing back to my target allocations?

If you decide you would rather spend your time with other aspects of life and hire an advisor because of the impact it can have, that choice will be one of the most important decisions you will ever make. Thus, it is critical you get it right. With that in mind, the following advice is offered.

There are four criteria which I have discussed throughout this book which should be absolutes when searching for the right advisor:

1. **A fiduciary standard of care.** A fiduciary versus a commission person is not only somebody who has the client's best interest in mind but will not do something *not* in the client's best interest even at the risk of losing the client. A fee-only advisor helps ensure the advice you receive is client-centric, not product-centric. You can even go to FINRA.com and perform due diligence to make sure there are no conflicts of interest.
2. **The advisor invests their own capital in the same way being recommended.** In other words does the advisor eat their own cooking and strictly follow the same principles they propose with their own personal assets? The investment vehicles and types of investments should be the same.

The advisor should submit to the same rigorous financial discipline they are suggesting for you.
3. **The advice is based on science (evidence based on peer reviewed journals) not opinions.** Know where your advice is coming from. Academic based wisdom provides confidence over opinionated ideas hands down.
4. **The firm integrates investment planning into a holistic financial plan.** A portfolio is not a plan. Consider the advisor a quarterback of the financial team., coordinating the efforts of every aspect of the plan. A good advisor will review everything on a regular basis.

Other ways a good financial advisor should add value is through regular ongoing communication, especially during times of crisis. Education can also prevent emotions from taking control over your portfolio. Helping explain complex financial products and processes in simplistic terms can be critical to keep investors disciplined and avoid costly mistakes.

It is critical to verify the advisor has appropriate credentials demonstrating knowledge and expertise in financial planning. Ensure they are current with required professional development. Lastly, it is also important that the advisor will deliver a high level of personal attention and develop strong personal relationships. This should be part of your due diligence process as you check the advisor's reputation from other professionals and client references.

The choice of a financial advisor is one of the most important decisions you will ever make. The bottom line is that you should choose one where the science of investing meets true wealth management, and that the services are delivered in a highly professional manner.

CHAPTER 16

NOW... THE CHOICE IS YOURS

Thank you for sticking with me this far. I realize I have given you a lot of information! Now you have some choices to make after considering everything you have read. From my experiences with others just like you, I think you have three choices.

First, you can stick your head in this door, look around, inhale once or twice and either recoil in horror or run like the wind to a more comfortable place that appears to be softer, gentler, kinder and less demanding. You may visit one promising option after another for years to come as you have in the past without choosing any of them. If that is your decision, it is okay with me. You may not be ready.

Second, you can join me and hang around a bit. Be casual, sampling a little of this... a little of that... not committing completely to the process and continue to wander leaving the door open to finding an even softer spot. If you do that you will pick up a few things without trying and maybe enough to surprise you with adequate results that cause you to move yourself from "casual and curious" to "committed and determined" over time. That's fine with me, too.

Or third, you can take this very, very seriously, still have fun, but principally go to work. Go to work at getting up to speed as quickly as possible, at understanding, and using every resource and implement, implement, implement.

We start with simple results and soon expand to bigger, more extensive and expansive complete holistic planning transformation. I won't lie. You have to dedicate some time, think it through, and focus. But it can quickly lead to a better place than where you are now.

Although this book has been pretty dry you'll actually find I am an amusing and entertaining fellow. I know lots of interesting people, famous and not so famous, and I like to tell stories and am fascinated with the absurdities and ironies in life. I enjoy sharing them with my clients in various newsletters and other correspondence I provide regularly.

Many clients have expressed delight in hearing my next discovery, my next rant or adventure as Tin Man with my granddaughter. You will have some fun here unless you're dull and incapable of fun.

These methods are academically based and proven to work through good times and bad by standing the test of time. Your plan should serve you as master and fulfill your financial and personal goals. Or do you believe you will get there at a satisfying pace just continuing as you are?

Are you sincerely motivated to create peace of mind, security and assure yourself you will not run out of money before you run out of life? Are you progressive, open-minded, and ready to reject limiting beliefs in favor of more effective ideas and strategies—or like Bilbo Baggins and afraid of adventure? Are you intrigued about financial freedom? Can you accept and act on experience-based advice and coaching?

I'll be honest. I'm not a good fit for everyone. But if you become my client and accept me as your guide, mentor, coach and advisor, I will prove to you the value of working with me.

Clearly you have time to address this most important issue. I must warn you that decisions tend to dissipate into nothingness without prompt action. It is better to put into motion the beginning of a plan while you're thinking about it.

I have one last thing to say. There are two categories of experience. Your own and other people's. Truthfully, I think there are some things that can only be learned through your own experience, but most investment success and strategies can best be acquired at reasonable costs through other people's experience.

The question really is not whether it's smart, efficient, and cost efficient to capitalize on the experience of others. The only real question is who do you want to get experience from? If you decide I am someone whose experience is valuable and important, I'm here to work with you.

A lot of my clients have made that decision. I have a great retention record to prove it. I want to share all my experience and information with you. It isn't something you should take lightly or be too busy to welcome.

Ready for the next step? Contact our office at 1-304-375-3843 to schedule a low-key conversation. It will allow me to get to know you and your financial goals while sharing more information customized to your needs.

Financial planning isn't something you want to put off. Make the call today. See for yourself if we're as dependable and full of integrity as this book has described. Your retirement dreams await.

I wish you the best in whatever you decide,

Sam

**Just to say thanks for reading my book,
I have a free toolkit
(including all the worksheets) you can download!
For your bonuses, go to:
www.smartretirementmadesimple.com**

www.ingramcontent.com/pod-product-compliance
Lightning Source LLC
Chambersburg PA
CBHW071501220526
45472CB00003B/881